Deadly Disasters

World's Worst EARTHQUAKES

Janey Levy

PowerKiDS press.

New York

Published in 2009 by The Rosen Publishing Group, Inc.
29 East 21st Street, New York, NY 10010

First Edition

Editor: Nicole Pristash
Book Design: Greg Tucker
Photo Researcher: Jessica Gerweck

Photo Credits: Cover © Marc Solomon/Getty Images; pp. 5, 15 Shutterstock.com; pp. 7, 17 © Getty Images; p. 9 © Gary Hincks/Photo Researchers, Inc.; p. 11 © Robert Yager/Getty Images; p. 12–13 © Dario Mitidieri/Getty Images; pp. 19, 21 © AFP/Getty Images.

Library of Congress Cataloging-in-Publication Data

Levy, Janey.
  World's worst earthquakes / Janey Levy. — 1st ed.
     p. cm. — (Deadly disasters)
  Includes index.
  ISBN 978-1-4042-4513-6 (lib. bdg.) ISBN 978-1-4042-4537-2 (pbk)
ISBN 978-1-4042-4555-6 (6-pack)
  1. Earthquakes—Juvenile literature. I. Title.
  QE521.3.L479 2009
  551.22—dc22
                                    2008007747

Manufactured in the United States of America

Contents

An earthquake is a shaking of the ground when Earth's **plates** suddenly break and move. **Scientists** think that more than 8,000 small earthquakes happen every day, but we do not feel most of them. Powerful earthquakes are uncommon. However, they can cause great **damage**.

An earthquake shook the Southeast Asian country of Indonesia in December 2004. It was one of the most powerful earthquakes in history. This earthquake caused a giant ocean wave, called a tsunami, that killed almost 230,000 people. Many other powerful earthquakes have happened throughout history. They have killed **millions** of people and destroyed cities.

The 2004 Indonesian earthquake caused several tsunami waves that came ashore and washed many villages away. This building was destroyed by the huge waves.

Where Do Earthquakes Happen?

Most earthquakes happen along **faults** on the edges of Earth's plates. Sometimes the moving plates push so hard that they bend rock along a fault. Continued pushing makes the rock break and move suddenly. This movement is an earthquake.

Most big earthquakes happen in a band around the Pacific Ocean. This band is called the Ring of Fire.

Earthquakes may also happen at soft spots in the middles of the plates. These earthquakes are not as strong as the ones that happen along faults. Sometimes earthquakes happen near **volcanoes**, too. Hot, melted rock moving under a volcano may cause an earthquake.

These wavy lines mark where the San Andreas Fault lies in Southern California. Earthquakes and plate movements cause the ground to move, which makes these lines in the ground.

Most earthquakes start deep inside Earth. The point where the rock first breaks is called the focus. The epicenter of an earthquake is the spot on Earth's **surface** right above the focus.

The break spreads along the fault. Sometimes one side of the fault drops below the other side. Sometimes one side moves up and over the other side. Other times the two sides slide past each other. The breaking rock lets out **energy** that travels through Earth in **seismic** waves. Waves that travel deep inside Earth are called body waves. Surface waves are waves that travel along Earth's surface.

This picture shows the movement of a strike-slip fault during an earthquake. At a strike-slip fault, two plates move against each other, making energy waves that cause the ground to move.

9

Earthquakes can cause a lot of damage. The breaking rock and seismic waves can tear up **structures** and roads, shake them, or cause them to fall. Structures can kill people when they fall and break. Earthquakes on the bottom of the ocean can cause tsunamis. Tsunamis knock down structures and cause very bad flooding. People can drown in the tsunamis as well.

There may be no food or clean water after an earthquake. Damaged roads and bridges may make it hard for help to reach people. This type of terrible damage has happened many times throughout history.

An earthquake in Mexico caused the top half of this building to fall onto the street below.

Pages 12–13: An earthquake turned this street onto its side in Osaka, Japan.

13

The deadliest earthquake in history happened over 800 years ago. A powerful earthquake struck the area around the eastern Mediterranean Sea in July 1201.

It is hard to know exactly what happened so long ago. Scientists have studied the records to learn all they can. They believe this earthquake was one of many that struck the area in June and July 1201. Tsunamis resulted and many places suffered terrible damage. More than one million people died. Most of the deaths were in the area that is now the countries of Egypt and Syria. No other earthquake ever recorded has killed so many people.

This is modern-day Cairo, Egypt. Cairo is in a place that was hit very hard by the Mediterranean Sea earthquake of 1201.

15

A powerful earthquake shook San Francisco, California, on April 18, 1906. No one knows for sure how strong it was. During that time, scientists did not have the tools needed to measure the **magnitude** of an earthquake. Some scientists today think it had a magnitude of 8, which is very powerful.

The San Francisco earthquake started fires that burned for three days. The earthquake and fires destroyed most of the city. The cost of the damage was about $500 million. About 3,000 people died, and about 250,000 people were left homeless. It was one of the worst **disasters** in U.S. history.

This picture was taken after the San Francisco earthquake in 1906. Here you can see the remains of some of the city's buildings, many of which were totally destroyed.

17

The 2004 Indonesian Earthquake

One of the most powerful earthquakes ever shook Indonesia on December 26, 2004. Scientists call it the Indonesian earthquake or the Sumatra-Andaman earthquake. It happened in the Indian Ocean near Sumatra, Indonesia.

This earthquake had a magnitude between 9 and 9.3. The fault was on the ocean bottom, and the break was about 850 miles (1,400 km) long. A huge tsunami resulted. It traveled thousands of miles (km) and hit 14 countries. The tsunami caused most of the deaths and damage. It washed away villages and about 230,000 people died. Almost two million people were left homeless.

After the Indonesian tsunami, many buildings were left with only their shells, like part of the building shown here.

19

If you live in an area where there are strong earthquakes, there are things you can do to keep safe. Stand in a doorway inside a building, or get under a strong table or chair. Stay there until the shaking stops. Be careful when you go outside and stay away from damaged structures.

Today, scientists know where earthquakes may happen. They have tools that help them measure ground movements. Still, scientists cannot say exactly when an earthquake will happen. People must be smart. Using these tips will help you stay safe during and after an earthquake.

This man is a seismologist. A seismologist studies earthquakes and other movements inside Earth. He is checking a seismograph, which is a machine that measures ground movements.

Earthquake Facts

One of history's deadliest earthquakes killed about 830,000 people in 1556, in Shaanxi, China. This earthquake's magnitude was at least 8.

A powerful earthquake happened in 1976 near Tangshan, China. This earthquake killed between 255,000 and 655,000 people. Almost 800,000 people were hurt.

The strongest earthquake in history happened off Chile's coast in 1960. This earthquake's magnitude was 9.5. Thousands of people died, and two million people became homeless.

The strongest earthquake ever recorded in the United States struck Alaska in 1964. This earthquake's magnitude was 9.2.

Glossary

damage *(DA-mij)* Hurt done to buildings, roads, trees, and belongings.

disasters *(dih-ZAS-terz)* Things that cause suffering or loss.

energy *(EH-nur-jee)* The power to work or to act.

faults *(FAWLTS)* Narrow breaks along the edges of Earth's plates.

magnitude *(MAG-nih-tood)* The size of something.

millions *(MIL-yunz)* Very large numbers.

plates *(PLAYTS)* The moving pieces of Earth's crust, the top piece of Earth.

scientists *(SY-un-tists)* People who study the world.

seismic *(SYZ-mik)* Caused by an earthquake.

structures *(STRUK-cherz)* Buildings, bridges, or roads.

surface *(SER-fes)* The outside of anything.

volcanoes *(vol-KAY-nohz)* Openings in the surface of Earth that sometimes send up a hot, melted rock, called lava.

Index

Web Sites

Due to the changing nature of Internet links, PowerKids Press has developed an online list of Web sites related to the subject of this book. This site is updated regularly. Please use this link to access the list:
www.powerkidslinks.com/disast/equake/